Before using these books...

☞ A teacher/counselor manual is separately available for guiding students in the use of these workbooks.

✎ To prevent bleed-through, it is recommended that water-based, rather than spirit-based, markers or pens be used in this workbook.

Important

This book is not intended as a treatment tool or to be utilized for diagnostic or investigative purposes. It is not designed for and should not be recommended or suggested for use in any unsupervised, self-help or self-therapy setting, group or situation. Professionals who use this book are exercising their own professional judgement and take full responsibility for doing so.

The STARS LifeSkills Program

Teacher/Counselor Manual

Learning About Anger

Learning More About Anger

Knowing Yourself

Getting Along with Others

Respecting Others

How Drugs and Alcohol Affect Us

Learning About Anger

Jan Stewart
Illustrated by Cecilia Bowman

ISBN 978-1-63026-835-0

© 2003 Jan Stewart and Hunter House
Design and layout Jinni Fontana © 2003 Hunter House
First U.S. edition published in 2003 by Hunter House.

For further information, contact Hunter House, Inc.

STARS: Steps to Achieving Real-life Skills

Learning About Anger

Dear Student:

This workbook is part of a program to help you learn some real-life skills. You may already have some of these skills, and the information may just be a reminder or a review. If the information is new to you, then it is possible for you to learn skills and strategies that can help you for the rest of your life.

If you are unable to complete any section, leave it blank and come back to it later. If you are still unsure, ask your parent or guardian to assist you. If this is not possible, ask the person who gave you the workbook. On the next page there is a glossary of words that are used in the workbook. Read this before you begin.

Please remember to have your parent or guardian fill out the last page.

Thank you for your cooperation.

Name of Student: _____

Adviser: _____

Assignment Date: _____

Completion Date: _____

Glossary

Antecedent — something that happens before something else

Anxious — feeling tense or nervous

Behavior — the way someone acts

Belittled — made to feel small or unworthy

Consequence — the result (of your behavior)

Humiliated — shamed or disrespected by others

Insecure — lacking confidence

Provoke — irritate or push someone

Relaxation Technique — a skill or activity you can use to calm yourself

Response — a reaction or answer using actions or words

Self-talk — words or phrases you say to yourself

Technique — a method or way of doing something

Tension — a feeling of stress, strain, or anxiety

Triggers — situations, events, or behavior that provoke or activate your anger

The STARS LifeSkills Program ★ Learning About Anger   ©2003 Jan Stewart and Hunter House, Inc.

Learning About Anger

Everyone gets angry some time during his or her life. Being angry is okay. But it is important to handle your anger, and not let it sneak up on you and get out of control. How you express anger can either be harmful or healthy. Handling anger means recognizing when you are beginning to get angry and then cooling yourself down. Sometimes people hurt themselves or others when they are angry; sometimes people keep their anger bottled up. Being in control of your feelings is hard work. With some effort, you can learn some important information and practical skills that you can use for the rest of your life. Knowing how to control your anger is a very powerful skill.

No one can make you control your anger. Only you can make the decision to be in control. Knowing about anger and practicing skills to manage anger will give you more control.

What is your definition of anger?

Anger is _____

_____

_____

_____

_____

Look up the word "anger" in a dictionary and write the definition here.

_____

_____

_____

_____

_____

Use the next page to draw a picture of anger.

Draw a picture that represents anger for you.

The STARS LifeSkills Program ★ Learning About Anger   ©2003 Jan Stewart and Hunter House, Inc.

Anger is an emotion that we see on the outside of a person; however, what is inside the person might be different. Because anger can flare up so quickly, it tends to hide other feelings such as hurt, fear, or jealousy. **Unscramble the words below and write the answers on the lines provided.**

_____ jecedrte

_____ radafi

_____ dsa

_____ fetl tou

_____ eursnu

_____ plslsehe

_____ soxiuna

_____ ltdetible

_____ secnireu

_____ hys

_____ muhliideta

_____ ratehteedn

_____ padisptnoied

_____ dfurtsrtae

Anger Triggers

Triggers are things that happen to your body to let you know you are getting angry. Some people feel lots of things and some only feel a few. Some common triggers are:

- Clenched jaw

- Tight muscles

- Sweating

- Red face

- Tight shoulders

- Shaking

- Butterflies in the stomach

- Rigid posture

- Hands clenched (in fists)

Whatever your triggers are, they act as clues for you to know that you are getting angry and that it is time to take control.

The STARS LifeSkills Program ★ Learning About Anger   ©2003 Jan Stewart and Hunter House, Inc.

Using the outline below, draw a picture of how you might look when you are angry. Write down *your triggers* under the picture. Finish the rest of the body and add any new lines you would like.

Your Triggers

_____

_____

_____

Problem Identification

Think about the last time you had a conflict or a problem. **Fill out the rest of this sheet to the best of your ability.**

Name: _____

Date: _____ ☐ Morning   ☐ Afternoon   ☐ Evening

What happened to cause the conflict or problem? _____

_____

_____

_____

Where were you? _____

What were you thinking? _____

_____

What did you do? Was there a positive or negative consequence? _____

_____

How did you handle yourself?

1	2	3	4	5
Poorly	Not so well	Okay	Good	Great

How angry were you?

1	2	3	4	5
Extremely angry	Really angry	Moderately angry	Mildly angry	Not at all angry

Did you feel any other emotion? If yes, what did you feel? _____

_____

_____

8

The STARS LifeSkills Program ★ Learning About Anger   ©2003 Jan Stewart and Hunter House, Inc.

The Anger Thermometer

What seems to make you angry? Imagine a thermometer. Zero would be something that doesn't make you angry at all. Ten would be something that would make you the angriest. Five would make you moderately angry. What are your levels? **Fill in the blanks next to the thermometer with events in your life that you get angry about.**

10 _____
(the angriest)

7.5 _____

5 _____
(moderately angry)

2.5 _____

0 _____
(not angry at all)

Where are you most of the time when you seem to get angry? **Put a check beside the place where you seem to get angry most of the time. Put an X by the place that is the second and put an O beside the place where you get angry the least.**

1. Home _____   2. School _____   3. With friends _____

Three Types of Anger

There are three ways that people generally express their anger: aggressively, passively, and assertively.

Aggressive anger:	Involves demanding your rights without thinking about the rights of others.
	This type of anger hurts people either emotionally, physically, or psychologically.
Aggressive people...	Blame others.
	Use physical or verbal violence.
	Bully or push people around.
	Yell or scream at others.
Passive anger:	Involves keeping your anger inside, and not dealing with the issue.
	This anger could result in feeling like you want to get even.
	Examples of passive anger include not talking to the other person, spreading rumors, and damaging people's property.
Passive people...	Make excuses.
	Don't want to express themselves.
	Blame themselves.
Assertive anger:	Involves standing up for your own rights and, at the same time, respecting the rights of others.
	This type of anger is expressed directly and in a non-threatening way to the other person involved.
Assertive people...	Use a variety of techniques to respond to anger.
	Express their feelings and thoughts to others.
	Are honest with themselves and others

Assertive people have the best results!

The STARS LifeSkills Program ★ Learning About Anger   ©2003 Jan Stewart and Hunter House, Inc.

At Home

☐ Passive ☐ Assertive ☐ Aggressive

At School

☐ Passive ☐ Assertive ☐ Aggressive

Out with Friends

☐ Passive ☐ Assertive ☐ Aggressive

The following are situations where someone gets angry. **Write on the line whether the anger is assertive, aggressive, or passive.**

1. Kareem is late for practice, so he yells at his mom while on the way there.

   _____

2. Serena honestly tells Chris that she doesn't feel like going with him to the game.

   _____

3. Luis gives Glen the excuse that he has to work, but Glen knows Luis isn't because he and John are going to a movie. They just don't want Glen along.

   _____

4. Win punched Karla because she heard from a friend that Karla called her a name.

   _____

5. Jamal tells Maria that he feels hurt when she calls him a loser and he wants her to stop.

   _____

6. Kim sits all alone and doesn't say anything when her friend ignores her.

   _____

If you get angry often, then it must have some advantages for you. Take some time to think about the advantages and the disadvantages of getting angry.

ADVANTAGES

(What good comes out of being angry?)

_____

_____

_____

_____

_____

_____

_____

DISADVANTAGES

(What bad comes out of being angry?)

_____

_____

_____

_____

_____

_____

_____

_____

The STARS LifeSkills Program ★ Learning About Anger   ©2003 Jan Stewart and Hunter House, Inc.

Relaxing

Just like people have their own triggers, they also have their own ways to relax or calm down. Some people go for a run, others for a swim. Some read a book, sit alone, or talk to their friends. What positive things could you do to calm yourself down when you are angry? Fill in all of your ideas into the pool below.

Self-Talk

Sometimes saying things inside your head will help reduce tension. Your words will help you to slow down and gain more control so that you can think clearly and act appropriately. Remember, you are the only one who can hear your words.

Some examples people use are

- Cool down

- Take it easy

- Get in control

- It isn't worth it

- Don't lose it.

People repeat these phrases in their head to help them cool down. They find this helpful when they're getting provoked or pushed around. When they feel their triggers, they use these words to relax. **Fill in the bubble with self-talk that could help someone cool down.**

The STARS LifeSkills Program ★ Learning About Anger   ©2003 Jan Stewart and Hunter House, Inc.

Interview

1. How do you know when you are getting angry?

_____

_____

_____

2. What do you do to relax or cool down?

_____

_____

_____

3. What words would you use for self-talk?

_____

_____

_____

4. What do you believe is the best thing to do when you're really angry?

_____

_____

_____

5. How did you learn to control your anger?

_____

_____

_____

Learning to Relax and Get Control

Deep Breaths

Have you ever watched an athlete waiting to run a race? How about a boxer in a boxing ring? Athletes practice taking **deep breaths** to relax themselves.

This is called a **relaxation technique.** It helps reduce tension and lets you focus on taking control of the situation. Taking deep breaths also gives you some time to make the right choice about handling your anger. People can use this technique to get control when they notice their triggers. When they're in control, they respond to anger in a positive way.

When someone is calling you names or pushing you around, getting control of yourself by taking deep breaths will help you respond in an assertive way.

Take a deep breath through your nose, hold it in for a couple of seconds, and then slowly let it out. Some people shut their eyes while they do this. Don't forget to use your self-talk when you use this technique.

Try taking a few deep breaths on your own right now.

What was this like for you?

_____

_____

_____

_____

_____

If you didn't notice any difference, don't worry because not every technique will work for everyone. Maybe another one will work.

The STARS LifeSkills Program ★ Learning About Anger   ©2003 Jan Stewart and Hunter House, Inc.

Assertion Techniques

Learning how to stand up for your rights and, at the same time, respecting the rights of others.

Strategy 1: The Skipping CD

This is when you say something over and over again with a calm tone of voice. You don't raise your volume, just repeat what you want over and over.

Here is an example of when to use it:

> If someone takes something of yours say, *"Please give me back my radio…Give me back my radio…Give me back my radio…"*

When could you also use this strategy?

_____

_____

_____

_____

_____

What would you say?

_____

_____

_____

_____

_____

Strategy 2: Friendly Reflection

This involves really listening to someone, and trying to guess how they must be feeling and then reflecting it back to them to let them know that you understand. This is a good method to use when someone with authority, like a parent or a teacher, is angry with you.

Here is an example of when to use it:

If you come home late and your parents are really mad, you could say: *"It sounds like you're really mad."* Or you could say: *"I know you're really mad at me for being late."*

When is another time that you could use this strategy?

_____

_____

_____

_____

_____

What would you say?

_____

_____

_____

_____

_____

18

Strategy 3: The Elevator

This is a response that increases in intensity as needed in order to get what you want. Begin with a minor request, then elevate to a serious request.

Here is an example of when to use it:

> If someone has taken something that belongs to you, and they will not give it back.

At first ask,

> *Please give my book back.*

Then, if they don't give it back you could say,

> *Give my book back.*

If they still don't cooperate, say,

> *I need my book back now.*

Finally, if they still have your book you could say,

> *If you don't give back my book, I will go to the teacher and she will get it for me.*

You can have more steps or levels to use depending on your patience level and how the other person reacts. What you say is as important as how you say it. Increasing your volume and becoming more serious with your tone of voice may be necessary if you want to get your point across and make sure the other person knows that you mean what you are saying.

Here is another example:

If you don't stop tapping me, I will go to the teacher!

Stop tapping me now!

I don't want you to tap me while I'm trying to work.

Please don't tap me while I work.

Start down here!

Try one of your own

Imagine:

A person in your class keeps on calling you a "loser" in front of someone you want to go out with. Using the elevator, fill in some responses you could use to get this person to stop.

Going Up

_____

_____

_____

_____

_____

_____

_____

_____

_____

_____

_____

_____

Start down here!

The STARS LifeSkills Program ★ Learning About Anger   ©2003 Jan Stewart and Hunter House, Inc.

Strategy 4: Short Circuit

This is a way to add humor to a situation and confuse the person who is provoking you.

Here is an example of when to use this:

If someone keeps putting you down, agree with that person and walk away.

This doesn't mean it's true, it's just a strategy to get that person to stop.

If someone says, *"You are stupid."* Say, *"You're right, I am stupid"* and walk away.

Remember, you're the one in control of the situation!

When is another time you could use this strategy? _____

_____

_____

What would they say? _____

_____

_____

What would you say? _____

_____

_____

Remember:

This is a good strategy to get you out of a situation that might get worse or have a negative consequence.

Strategy 5: "I" Messages

An "I" message is an assertive technique used to respond to someone trying to provoke you.
Here is the formula:

When you...

I feel...

because...

I need...

Here is how it might sound:

When you *take my book,*

I feel mad

because *I have to do my work.*

I need you to give it back.

Here is another example:

When you *call me names,*

I feel hurt

because *it embarrasses me.*

I need you to stop insulting me.

The STARS LifeSkills Program ★ Learning About Anger   ©2003 Jan Stewart and Hunter House, Inc.

1. Your brother borrowed your tape without asking and lost it.

When you _____

I feel _____

because _____

I need _____

2. Two of your friends are whispering behind your back and giggling at you.

When you _____

I feel _____

because _____

I need _____

3. Every time you walk by this certain person in the hallway, he or she pushes you into the lockers.

When you _____

I feel _____

because _____

I need _____

4. You just got your hair cut, and a person in your class told you it looks ugly and keeps making jokes about it.

When you _____

I feel _____

because _____

I need _____

5. Every time you answer incorrectly in class another student keeps calling you a "loser," "geek," or "idiot."

When you _____

I feel _____

because _____

I need _____

Remember:

Try to prevent yourself from losing control of your angry emotions.

The STARS LifeSkills Program ★ Learning About Anger   ©2003 Jan Stewart and Hunter House, Inc.

Strategy 6: Ignore

Walking away from someone who is trying to provoke you is another very useful strategy. It tells the other person that you are not willing to respond to him or her or that you need more time to think of an appropriate response to what he or she has said or done. You're the person in control of the situation. The hard part about this is that it takes a lot of courage and strength to walk away from someone who is provoking you. Remember your self-talk and give yourself positive messages like:

It's not worth it.

This person is the one with the problem, not me.

I'm stronger and have more control than them.

Physical fighting is for people who don't know any positive strategies.

The consequences for fighting are worse.

I can't be bothered.

Whatever statement works for you is the best. Talking silently to yourself helps distance you from the situation. Walking away takes a very strong person with a very strong mind. Always keep in mind what will occur if you act a certain way.

Think to yourself:

If I (behavior) now, then I will (consequence)."

For example:

"If I yell back at this teacher now then I will be on detention all lunch hour."

Sometimes people like to see others get angry. Often people push others until they lose control.

1. Have you ever told someone about a person who was picking on you?

    ☐ Yes   ☐ No

2. Did the person you tell suggest that you IGNORE the other person?

    ☐ Yes   ☐ No

3. Do you ever have a hard time ignoring someone who is bugging you?

    ☐ Yes   ☐ No

Ignoring someone is difficult. It takes a lot of patience to ignore someone who is bugging you. When you give in to someone who bugs you, you're giving them control. When you ignore someone, you are in control.

Take the quiz on the next page to find out how you react to different situations.

How much self-control do you have? How easy is it for you to ignore someone who is trying to get you angry? **Check the answer that best describes you.**

1. A student sitting behind you is whispering to you to get you to turn around while the teacher is talking.

    ☐ Easy to ignore ☐ Difficult to ignore ☐ Impossible to ignore

2. A friend is making weird faces at you to try to get you to laugh while the teacher is explaining something to you.

    ☐ Easy to ignore ☐ Difficult to ignore ☐ Impossible to ignore

3. A student in class throws paper at you.

    ☐ Easy to ignore ☐ Difficult to ignore ☐ Impossible to ignore

4. A person you don't know insults you.

    ☐ Easy to ignore ☐ Difficult to ignore ☐ Impossible to ignore

5. A person in class makes weird noises.

    ☐ Easy to ignore ☐ Difficult to ignore ☐ Impossible to ignore

The STARS LifeSkills Program ★ Learning About Anger   ©2003 Jan Stewart and Hunter House, Inc.

6. A person in class says something mean about your family.

   ☐ Easy to ignore   ☐ Difficult to ignore   ☐ Impossible to ignore

7. A person you've never met passes you on the street and calls you a racist name.

   ☐ Easy to ignore   ☐ Difficult to ignore   ☐ Impossible to ignore

8. A student is trying to get your attention while you are taking a test.

   ☐ Easy to ignore   ☐ Difficult to ignore   ☐ Impossible to ignore

9. The class clown is giving funny answers and the teacher is getting angry.

   ☐ Easy to ignore   ☐ Difficult to ignore   ☐ Impossible to ignore

10. A group of kids is teasing you about the way you dress.

    ☐ Easy to ignore   ☐ Difficult to ignore   ☐ Impossible to ignore

Calculate your score on next page . . .

Scoring

Give yourself 1 point for each "easy to ignore."

Give yourself 2 points for each "difficult to ignore."

Give yourself 3 points for each "impossible to ignore."

What is your total? _____

Use the following scale to see how you rate:

10–15 Wow! You keep control in many situations that could distract or anger people.

16–25 You have very good self-control. You can ignore things if you choose.

26–30 You choose not to ignore many things. With a bit of help, you can learn to ignore more things so that you feel more in control.

The STARS LifeSkills Program ★ Learning About Anger   ©2003 Jan Stewart and Hunter House, Inc.

Why is it sometimes difficult to ignore people who are bugging you?

Describe a situation when you should ignore someone. _____

_____

_____

_____

Describe a situation when you shouldn't ignore someone. _____

_____

_____

_____

Tips on how to ignore someone who is bugging you.

Imagine there is a big WALL between you and the person bugging you.
Each letter in WALL stands for a tip on how to ignore.

Walk away

Act like nothing is happening

Look away

Look like you are busy

When you ignore someone who is bugging you, you're in control of the situation. If you give in and get angry, the other person is in control.

Journal Writing–Reflecting

Take a moment to think about the work you have done in this workbook. **Jot down some words about how you felt working on this workbook.** From there, use a sentence starter to write about what you have accomplished. Pick the sentence starter that you like and write a paragraph about anything you want. This is a chance for you to be creative and to write something for yourself. Use the space below and a separate sheet if necessary.

If you are better with pictures, feel free to draw a picture.

Sentence Starters

One thing that makes me very angry is...

Sometimes when I am angry I...

I need to _____ when I'm angry because...

When I am angry I feel...

_____

_____

_____

_____

_____

_____

_____

The STARS LifeSkills Program ★ Learning About Anger   ©2003 Jan Stewart and Hunter House, Inc.

Learning About Anger

Parents/Guardians

It would be helpful if you could review and comment on the work that your child has done in this workbook. We encourage students to work with their parents on certain sections and we thank you for your cooperation. We hope that your child has had a chance to examine their behavior and to plan positively for the future. This unit has exposed students to a lot of information which we hope could be reviewed at home. We greatly appreciate your partnership in this project.

Comments: _____

_____

_____

_____

_____

_____

Please feel free to contact the student's advisor or the person who assigned this workbook if you have any other questions or concerns.

Students

Now that you have completed the workbook, we urge you to provide some comments. Please comment on anything positive, e.g. "What did you like about it?" Also comment on what you did not like. If you have any suggestions, we would also like to hear them. **Congratulations for all your hard work!**

Comments: _____

_____

_____

_____

_____

_____

The STARS LifeSkills Program ★ Learning About Anger   ©2003 Jan Stewart and Hunter House, Inc.